AMBUSH A̶  ̶̶̶̶̶  ̶ɛ

Caroline Bird's selected poems, *Rookie* (2022), and *The Air Year* (2020) are two of Carcanet's most popular books of the present decade. She won the Forward Prize for Best Collection in 2020, and has been shortlisted for a number of prizes including the T.S. Eliot Prize, the Costa Book Awards, the Ted Hughes Award, the Polari Prize and the Dylan Thomas Prize. A two-time winner of the Foyle Young Poets Award, her first collection *Looking Through Letterboxes* was published in 2002 when she was fifteen. She won a Cholmondeley Award in 2023.

CARCANET POETRY PRESENTS

# AMBUSH AT STILL LAKE

## poems by
### CAROLINE BIRD

First published in Great Britain in 2024 by
Carcanet
Alliance House, 30 Cross Street
Manchester, M2 7AQ
www.carcanet.co.uk

A CIP catalogue record for this book is
available from the British Library.

ISBN 978 1 80017 412 2

Book design by Andrew Latimer, Carcanet
Typesetting by LiteBook Prepress Services
Printed in Great Britain by SRP Ltd, Exeter, Devon

The publisher acknowledges financial
assistance from Arts Council England.

# CONTENTS

*'Just when the water was settled and at home'*

– Richard Hugo

# AMBUSH AT STILL LAKE

## THE STANDSTILLER

I pick up my souvenir photo.
Unruffled hair. A steady gaze.
'Wait, so it literally doesn't move?'
you ask, windswept from the dodgems.
'Not a millimetre!' I say, re-joining
the queue. You suggest the Eternal
Abyss Turbo Plunge instead.
'Trust me,' I say, 'This one's scarier.'
I steer us onto the wheelless train
but, at the last moment, you panic
and bail. 'I'll be right here
on the platform,' you say, waving
as the restraints come down and off
I go, staying beside you.

## DREAM JOB

The three-year-old boss
of our imaginary café
is conducting his daily stocktake.
'Cabbages? Yes. Chocolate? Yes.
Carrots...?'
He looks around, consults
his palm like a clipboard.
'Here you are,' I say, magicking
a bunch from my pocket,
'Fresh and crunchy.'
He stares at me.
'That's not carrots,' he says,
'That's nothing.'
So it is. Business suffers.
No pretend biscuits. No pretend milk.
I ring up our wholesale distributor.
The dial tone is fuzzy, fleshy.
'That's not a phone, that's your hand.'
Fuck. I've made international calls
from that number, lucrative deals –
yesterday we sold pizzas,
horses, islands, trains
with personalised *choo-choos*.
You name it, we had it.
Now, suddenly, the opposite.
Peas? No. Eggs? No. Chicken? No.
It's an emptying, an exodus.
Invisible shelves all bare.
Already I can picture a throng
of disgruntled customers,
banging down our doors

shouting 'Call *this* a tomato?'
demanding refunds
when the money just isn't there
and the boss, he's so calm,
poking playdoh in his office
like he's been fudging discrepancies
in the books for some time,
watching his Ponzi scheme crash
and pretty soon, he knows
the nee-naws will come
and he'll turn to me, handcuffed
and say *wasn't it great*
*while it lasted though, Mum?*
*Didn't we want*
*for nothing?*

Nannie Edna couldn't accept that her dying wish was borderline psychopathic. 'But it's what I want!' she rasped through her breathing apparatus. We tried suggesting more conventional alternatives (swimming with dolphins, a hot air balloon ride, a video call with Michael Ball) but she wasn't interested. She wanted to dangle her great-grandson from her apartment window. 'By the ankle!' she kept saying, as if we might agree to let her dangle him by the arm and accidentally disappoint her. When we said no, she went through the five stages of grief. 'But I'm dying...?' and 'You don't trust me! You've never trusted me!' She lifted her heavy handbag and held it in the air, shaking, for a good five minutes: 'See? I wouldn't drop him.' We didn't know what to say. Tears ran sideways down her face. Finally, she closed her eyes. 'My own family believes I am capable of dropping a newborn baby from a twelve-storey building and, deep down, I suppose, I've always known this about myself,' she said, slipping away.

## ANTS

The cereal cupboard is alive
with errant mannerisms
like droplets of coffee in space

shaped like the dark apertures
of tiny keyholes.
Truant crochets

who bunked off their orchestral scores
to avoid being reduced
to one note

and now silently roam the octaves
of tin and shelf
with no idea who they are.

I fix the crevice nozzle
to my vacuum cleaner
and switch it on.

Come on, you shrunken comet tails.
You mincing motes.
It's harvest time.

I open the cupboard door
like peeling back my scalp
to catch the lost neurons

and one by one, I pick them off.
Each laid bare and manic
like a toddler's scribble

made sentient by a tab of acid.
Think you're safe under the cat food?
Think again.

It's kinder than poison, I tell myself,
picturing them still lucid
in the hoover bag

upside down, hysterical
in the roaring dark.
And just when they think I'm finished

I come back for the stragglers
until my cupboard is clean
and my mind is in order

and I can finally leave
to collect my son from nursery
yet all the while I'm thinking

under the skirting boards,
a tin I didn't check,
the survivors are

fizzling, cold with relief.
They reunite by the Cheerios
to recover the bodies.

High and low, they search
an empty battlefield.
Not even a blackened smear,

an eyelash of a leg. It's as if
the sky just parted
and sucked their comrades in.

They hold a meeting,
speak pheromonally
of the rapture

when the black hole opened
and they were not chosen
but left behind, wingless,

to continue in a Godless land
where lawlessness now has
the upper hand.

They didn't catch us in Burnt Spoon.
They didn't catch us in Catgut Valley,
Bigsip, Missionary Wharf, Trad Beach,
Cornice Creek, Keelova or Slip Ridge
and the rewind boy at the Hippodrome
in Log Port never could describe my lips
or your nose to the police sketch artist
because we didn't go back. *Let me dance
with you in Still Lake one more time* I said
– or was it you? – sluicing off the blood
in some nameless field. Meanwhile,
a red-faced man found a prescription
in a stolen car, called in the address and
two weeks later, our Buick self-drove
her last getaway into a ditch. So many
Bobs and Bills and Bruces who couldn't
wait to say, 'I was there. In the bushes.'
4am is the worst hour to get arrested
as it counts for yesterday and today – but
getting shot a hundred times in bursts
of machine gun fire, just before dawn,
500 yards from Still Lake? We carry on
dying forever, always almost home.

## A SHAKEN LEAF

I saw a horror movie once
where nothing happened.
Or, the *trees* did it?
One minute, families
swung tote bags
under hawthorn blossom,
a pink trainer steadied the deck
of a tasselled scooter
then BAM!
the grass fluttered,
a centipede paused,
a milking stool fell on its side
and Mark Wahlberg
grabbed his kid and ran.
From what? All we knew
was the sound of a shaken leaf
would chase them
till all their sanctuaries
be laid desolate
like the day we took the boy
to the National Trust Gardens
and did not forget
his wellies nor his cup.
Free parking. Grazing deer.
My glove in your glove
then BAM!
the grass fluttered,
a bullfrog croaked,
his buggy harrumphed on a clod
and you left your body,
I was suicidal, he wanted

hot chocolate but the café
was fucking miles away
and we were never
ever, ever
going to make it.

When they arrive, we can't tell
whether they've paid by gold card
or court order or health insurance
or Hollywood relatives or the last
of their savings. Clues like urine
soaked jeans or flashy coats
are often false leads. We can't tell
what car they drive, if they have kids
that still call them. Everyone rocks up
at random times. 4am. Breakfast.
One guy strolls in for Christmas
dinner, loads a plate with shrimp
he doesn't eat, his pupils like distant
stars blinking through cloud.
We call them 'the new people.'
*Have you seen that new person?*
Paul. Baseball cap. Rope-mark
round his neck like a strip of sunburn.
Nothing else to him. At first,
they live in glimpses, a shaking head
at the nurses' window, tongues
extended like flayed palms.
You can barely talk to a new person.
One woman takes five minutes
to tell us she's a 'respiratory therapist.'
'That's cool,' we say, wishing she'd
shut up. Details feel dirty. We don't
want the dawn needling in the blinds,
stretching our shadows, illuminating
white capsule-specks in our turds
but we can't stop it. And even if

one night we find a rolled-up tenner
in our pyjama pocket that's beaten
the bag search and lick it clean,
it won't make us new again. Unless
we're new forever like the postman
with wet brain who 'cannot be helped'
or the heart-scar girl with a face like
old snow and a death wish to clinch
back in Aspen. Mostly, we return to
ourselves, platelet by platelet, until
the minibus pulls up and we collect
our phones and shoelaces and razors
from the entrance desk on steady legs
and say 'excuse me' as we pass a new
person arriving with that bleachy hum
rising from the floorboards of their skin
and for a second The Future eyeballs
The Past but neither can tell who's who.

## STICK PARENT

Crayon oozes out over the lines
of myself. 'Wow,' a voice says,
'Now *that* is art!' I look around:
nothing but the thick blue stripe
of the sky. My triangular house.
The flat grass. 'It's so good,'
says the voice, 'Let's stick it on
the fridge.' I feel my world lift
then darken as a giant magnet
clamps the sun. I smile through
my eye dots. I'm art. I'm good.

Tasha was allergic to rain. It made her heart muscles droop
and stretch, and fattened her liver. Then the rain stopped

and she collapsed, shaking like a vibrator let loose
on a hard tiled floor. She was allergic to not-rain too.

On snowy days, guess what? Night sweats, ghastly dreams
of crusty brown avalanches, and when the sun came out

her faeces turned white. She lay in a sealed floatation tank
and puked all over the UV lights. She was allergic to air-

conditioned rooms, crowds, silence and cars. Children
made her fall into the road. 'This is ridiculous,' she thought,

setting off to search the world for one thing that didn't leave
her sick and tired. She staged experiments: clutching a beetroot

as blood vessels burst in her face, admiring a bluebell
till her gut leaked. Finally, she wound up in a reverted chapel

bar called The Old Creamery, full of kitsch twig racks
and sustainably harvested wooden beams. She drank

twelve martinis. The waiter had that uptalk speech, uprooting
each full-stop. 'Easy there?' he said. Tasha blinked slowly.

No tremors. What'd you know, it *was* easy there. Turns out,
she wasn't allergic to rustic modern interior design!

I was scrambling eggs when my baby brother rang.
'My flatmate is descended from King Louis XIV,' he said.

'Hello Peter.'

'He won't admit it but he's the spitting image
of the oil painting,' he said, 'And he's an absolutist,
I fucking hate absolutists
so I plan to recreate the dragonnades of 1681.'

'The dragon what?'

'I'll smash up his mugs and spit on his toothbrush
to avenge the Huguenots.'

I took the pan off the hob.

'Also,' he said, '*Jack the Clipper*,
eight-part miniseries, based on an unsolved case
of hair theft from 1923. I'll use exclusively bald actors,
even the horses will be bald – we'll shave the horses –
to make a point.'

'What point?'

'Also, the Royal Astronomical Society
need my guidance because Pluto IS a full-sized planet.'

It was 8am. 'PLUS,' he said, 'Top secret project, seven words:
Donald Rumsfield, Exhumation, Corpse Trial, Posthumous Hague.
Also, I've bought a pet chicken to test my dog's morals:
if my dog kills my chicken, I'll kill my dog.'

He stopped for breath.

'These all sound like excellent ideas, Peter.'

'Really?'

'You're ahead of the game.'

'Thanks Sis,' he said, sounding happy for the first time
since we were children,
'That means everything to me. I love you.'

'I love you too,' I said, hanging up.
Sis. He never called me that.
I returned the pan to the heat
with an extra knob of butter. 'Sissss...sisssss,'
said the eggs.

## THE BABY MONITOR

He snored. It screamed.
He laughed. It let out
this horrible throaty rattle.
I read it stories,
made a shoebox bed,
spooned macaroni into its ports
until it smelt like milky vomit
and I could never get it fully clean.
'I'm scared of you,' it said,
learning to talk, and 'You're a baddie.'
My boy reached 'rainbow level'
at preschool then 'pot of gold,'
tied his own laces
but I sat through parents' evening
like a killer in the dock, knowing
the monitor was home alone,
crying to an empty room.
No wonder its plastic
appeared blueish and dusky,
and rapid breathing woke me at 1am,
2am, 4am; that crackling plea:
'Where are you, Mum?'
like a boy floating in space
with a fading radio signal.
But what could I do?
Shrink myself to a particle?
Shave my skin down to pure
soundwave and climb up a wire?
Find it in death?
Maybe that's what it takes.
I don't remember pulling the plug

just the dull red bulb of its eye
then silence falling
but for the moan
of my son's clarinet lesson
slowly filling the house.

## THE BRIDES

When you agreed to marry me, I thought of the Babushkas
who journeyed home like salmon swimming to freshwater,

who crawled miles through bushes, dug under barbed wire
to get back to the Dead Zone just to drink their own water,

who kissed each other on the lips, exchanged Easter cakes,
became accustomed to a slight uranium taste in the water

despite the rusted Ferris wheel in idleness forever, despite
the relatives in vaulted wards with flesh like crimson water

dying nightly in their dreams. The Babushkas who brewed
moonshine from potatoes, yeast and seven gallons of water,

dried their buckets on branches, sat wide-legged on porches
as Geiger counters fizzed about the fields like boiling water

and camera-facing experts, holding conical flasks, explained
(again) that nothing was forgotten or forgiven by this water

yet chickens still clucked on impassable roads, gooseberries
glinted, sunlight passed through old curtains like pink water

and the Chernobyl Brides lived off that earth, refusing to die
till one hundred and five, as if touched by some magic water

or the forcefield in your eyes today, blessing a poisoned aisle
to say, 'I take thee, Caroline' in your dress like running water.

I was woken at 4am by a plainclothes police officer. 'I'm here to help!' she said, barging in. 'I think there's been some mistake,' I said. 'So many mistakes,' she said, nodding gravely. 'No... I meant...' She put her finger on my lips. 'It's quiet in your house. Eerie. Like a snooker hall inside a sunken cruise ship.' 'It's the middle of the night,' I said. She decanted my orthopaedic slippers into two plastic baggies, picked up my porcelain model of a cowhand and said, 'Oh dear' then asked me if I knew what a carburettor was. I didn't. She inspected my kitchen: 'Why do you have day-old meatballs in the fridge?' I couldn't answer. She pointed at a slightly open door and whispered, 'That's ajar.' I got an itchy feeling. Something *was* off. Why was that teabag there? What was that burnt bread smell within the bowels of my toaster? 'I intend to fully cooperate with your inquiries,' I said. Her radio grunted. 'I've got the wrong house.' She stood in the corner for ten minutes, muttering, unbagged my slippers then left, apologising. 'I do hope you find the right address,' I said, 'Whoever it is clearly needs a lot of help.' She shook her head. '4am was my only window. It'll be too late for them now.'

Since your sentencing, my online algorithm's
gone mad. This morning, it said *Perhaps
You'd Like* then suggested a two-inch, yellow
'Caution Wet Floor' sign for a doll's house.

I don't own a doll's house! I'm not worried
about miniature spillages, like a teardrop
in a living room, an older doll might slip on
for want of a tiny wet floor sign, am I?

Why would I be? It tells me customers
who viewed items in my browsing history
also viewed: bulk steel plating, wimples,
lightsaber chopsticks, bereavement cruises

and German reggae. Does that sound like me?
Who is this consumer of 1683 Swedish
Uniform Regulation History and balloon porn?
Sorry. You've got bigger things to bother about

than glitches in my personalised marketing.
Have you been reading? Are there AA meetings?
Do you have any idea what I might have done
to give myself these audio book recommendations?

My top four, apparently, are: '*Pus, a Guide
to the Aspiration of Abscesses,*' '*Managing a Flea Circus:
the Fidel Castro Way,*' '*Top 100 Saddest Chairs*'
and '*How to Please Your Man.*' I thought I was gay?

*Do* I like German Reggae? *Am* I attracted
to the wacky waving inflatable tube guy?
It gets darker. Perhaps I'd like to see a monkey
in a blender? Perhaps I'd like 200 plastic foetuses

for 'handing out at abortion clinics.' I don't, do I?
Tell me I don't. FOR YOU shouts the flashing
pop-up box, clicking open to reveal
a bludgeoned badger wearing lipstick. For me?

Really? *Click on this video!* I cover my eyes and
watch through my fingers, in case I'm against
what I'm into. Please don't be illegal, I think
as a young hand performs a length gyration

on The Classroom Friendly Pencil Sharpener.
Is this who I am behind closed doors? Perhaps
I'm the sort of person who purchases a bike desk
or knits cat jumpers from dog hair or writes

a character reference for a violent offender
saying 'this was out of character' even though
I wasn't there. But she was, wasn't she?
The one who filed the restraining order.

'She may also like' a bone fracture. 'She may
also like' a recurring nightmare, downloaded
to her retinas without her permission.
What do you dream about in prison? Last night

I was driving somewhere in the countryside
and I felt so free with my fragrant nodding gnome
stuck to the dashboard and my fragrant gnome
car ornament, swinging from my rear-view mirror.

Then I woke up. My wife said I kept mumbling
the tagline over and over. Fucking tech giants, man,
targeting our dreams. Why else would I be crying
every night for no reason, reaching out, repeating

*smells like gnome, smells like gnome, smells like gnome,*
*smells like gnome, smells like gnome, smells like gnome,*
*smells like gnome, smells like gnome, smells like gnome,*
*smells like gnome, smells like gnome, smells like gnome*

Uncle Stan has a lung thing.
Linda has a bladder thing.
Stew has an outcropping
of gangrenous fantails.
From a height, Jim's rash
resembles a 1922 postmark
and Lucy's nasal corkscrew
has dampened her bon viveur.
Since Mike's yo-yo diet,
his biceps have crumbled to crepe
paper and his teeth are tree-lined
with cabbage specks. Lance
spends his nights slow-waltzing
with a visitation, outside
the potholes brim with rain
like looted blisters and no-one's stomach
can hold so much as a water biscuit.
A backstreet surgeon jimmied Jen's
liver open with a pen-lid, now
she's flatspoken and wallpapered
in plum blossom bruises but
don't worry, she's dead-
set on designing the Order of Service
for your wedding on Saturday
and everyone will be there
except Gerald who found an ancient
paintball lodged in his left ventricle,
intact; the doctors say
it's holding him together
but he can't risk dancing
to Build Me Up Buttercup for fear of it

splattering inside him like a bullet
made of blood but he sends
forty quid (enclosed) and wishes you
a long and happy life together.

## GAG GIFT

Marlie brought home a lie detector
party game called 'OUCHY!'

The box said, 'A cool way
to make you sweat bullets.'

It was silver and plastic
and D-shaped like a robot vacuum cleaner

with five finger cavities
like battery chambers.

'It looks complicated,' I said.
'Nonsense,' she said,
'You simply strap in the player's hand
then ask a Yes/No question
like, do you like mushrooms?
Are you scared of spiders?'

She knew I hated mushrooms
and I wasn't scared of spiders.

The manual was in English and Mandarin.
I sat down with my coffee to read it cover to cover,

'*OUCHY has two types of punishment functions:
vibration and electric shock.*'

'What is this, Guantanamo?' I said.
'It's a gag gift,' she said,
opening the fridge with her foot
to grab the milk,

'I thought it would be a fun alternative
to charades on Christmas Day.'

Maybe I *was* scared of spiders.
Maybe I *didn't* hate mushrooms.

I remembered an article about a serial killer
with multiple personality disorder
who'd passed a polygraph by truly,
in that moment, believing himself
to be a different person altogether.
One of his 'alters' was a six-month-old baby.

Marlie flipped up her laptop
to type her vacation-response

and I fell to the floor, violently bawling.
'Oh my God, what's the matter?' she said, testing me
but I sucked my thumb, stayed in character.
Belief wasn't enough. I had to become

the baby. Remember the wallpaper.
Remember the bars of your cot.
Now shit yourself. Feel the texture.
All over your pyjamas. Cry
for Mummy. No, not you, I don't want you,
where's Mummy? I need her,
I've done a bad thing.

enjoys late-night call-ins
like 'Imminent Global Takeover'
and 'Resist Satan'
hosted by pink-necked men
who say, 'Where are you
calling from?' His leather recliner
sports a pull-out cup holder
and the leaflet on his pegboard
reads 'Immune System Booster
and Nootropic Brain
Supplements Mega Deal.'
He hears a click on the line
and knows someone is listening.
Aliens with an interest
in home phones and pegboards
and the lucent embassy of his mind.
'Dad, have you eaten?'
Yes, he says, certain
that next Sunday morning, she'll hear
his voicemail and he won't be in
the garden or napping
but ascending
on a rock to the mothership.

## SIBLINGS

A woman gave birth
to the reincarnation
of Gilbert and Sullivan
or rather, two reincarnations:
one Gilbert, one Sullivan.
What are the odds
of both being resummoned
by the same womb
when they could've been
a blue dart frog
and a supply teacher
on separate continents?
Yet here they were, squidged
into a tandem pushchair
with their best work
behind them, still smarting
from the critical reception
of their final opera
described as 'but an echo'
of earlier collaborations.

I whisper to each pill
*You are the Messiah.*
*Go forth.* They flume
my oesophagus, ready
to spread light, renovate
sewage systems, calm
my baying crowds with
their singular brand of
shtick. They start strong,
chanting psalms under
bronchiole willow trees
until, as per, their flash
cards get muddled and
sermons dissolve: *Um.*
*Thread needles through*
*the eyes of... rich camels?*
Booing ensues. I get ill.
Then it's all *Forgive me,*
*Lord! I have failed you!*
Incessant praying: *Give*
*us a true Messiah!* I try.
Now sleeping bags line
my stomach-streets like
cracked capsules, one
thousand dud redeemers
cooking undigested gum
on rusty propane stoves,
coughing and mourning
their blisterpack cribs;
that holy day when God
kissed the chalk circle

of their button mouths
and sent them down
a neck to save a world.

## THE BEST ROOM

The dinner service
gleams behind glass.

The knives and forks
align their pearl handles
like star-crossed lovers
in a green felt morgue.

A pheasant stares,
unshootable,
from the woodland scene
of a gilded plate.

The seats of the chairs
are bordered with beads
that know nothing of buttocks.

Behold, gravy boat.
Behold, ceramic pear.

Only shadows play in here.

The Ouzo from the long-ago
holiday to Corfu
will not be consumed
in this lifetime

and the snow-globes sit
oblivious
to the storm
sleeping inside them.

Everybody came to my first wedding.
Smelly Neil from primary school
played 'Splat the Rat' with the skinhead girl
who sold me fake ecstasy. The bodybuilders
from Dad's porn films told jokes about potatoes
to monochrome ancestors who'd perished
in the Great Famine. After dinner, the midwife
passed around the bloody forceps.
The 'absent friends' toast got a bit confusing
as they all kept piping up, 'I'm here!'
The line-up took hours, embracing every
half-remembered person: the man
from the secret photos in mum's dresser,
my teenage babysitter who jumped off a cliff
at Flamborough Head, etc. Some faces
were impossible to place. 'I'm sorry,' I said,
finally, to one chap, 'Who are you?'
He looked at me, hurt. 'I'm a BT operator,
I kept you in a call queue for forty minutes in 2007.'
'Of course,' I said. 'Listen,' he said,
'The band is playing our song!' And they were.
Greensleeves. Instrumental. Synthesized.
'Wow,' I said, 'It takes me right back
to being on hold with you.'
'I know,' he said, 'Isn't that extraordinary?'
and we danced together, reminiscing
under a marquee of stars.

## DOWNER

After his resurrection,
Dad was constantly exhausted
and all of his anecdotes were about soil.
He'd start a story with
'When I was dead...'
and everyone would groan.
It's hard to eat spaghetti carbonara
whilst discussing the nutrient-rich
properties of a corpse
especially when the speaker
keeps nodding off mid-sentence
then resuming with a start
like an animatronic fortune teller
with ill-fitting batteries
programmed purely to depress you
and we told him as much.
'Shut up, Dad, we don't want
any more of your soil stories.
One more soil story and we'll wish
you were dead again.'
He thought for a minute,
'I could talk about rhizomes?'
'What's a rhizome?' I said,
hoping for something scary or mystical.
'Creeping root-stalks in the...'
'Don't you dare say soil!'
Sandra slammed down her napkin, incensed,
then fled to the kitchen to bury
her ugly sobs in a tea-towel.
'Now look what you've done!'
but he'd fallen asleep

with his fingers in his ears
as was his strange new habit
as if *we* were the boring ones,
too consumed by our polka-dotted teapots
and satirical webisodes
to appreciate his tales
of indistinguishable muds
which had no doubt
enraptured the worms.

of an international scandal,
my son sees his own name
everywhere. R.
He has learnt to spell R.
He points at picture books.
Rat. Car. Green. 'That's my name!'
He points at film credits, chuffed
to be acknowledged. Director.
'That's my name!' Big R
looks like a dinosaur and little r
is a worm's head. He's on BBC News
before I switch the channel: Russia,
Tax Rate, Minister, Porn, War,
his name like a landmark lit up
in the fog. He's on posters, t-shirts,
every sign in the butterfly sanctuary;
a pintsize tycoon with stakes
in multiple businesses from Greggs
to The Ritz. He almost chokes
on his biscuit at the sight of 'Riverside
Leisure Centre.' He can't move for
mentions, it's a media frenzy, splashed
around indiscriminately: Father
Christmas, Warning Fragile Roof,
Beer, Jupiter, Lazar Hair Removal,
my wife's surname, step mother, his name
in my name, embedded, ubiquitous
until Sunday when I give him back
to his other mum like a bouncer
handing over my A-lister

to an elite security team
then going home to a quiet flat
crammed high with memorabilia.

## CHOKING HAZARD

She saw a TV show called 'Guess What's Inside Her?'
about an old lady who ate washing powder

then nibbled two-thirds of a three-seater sofa
and Martha felt *seen,* watching this, she felt lighter

because she'd had seventeen Troll Dolls for dinner.
It started with Lego, the odd Scrabble letter,

her excrement glittered with unicorn stickers.
In spite of bleach-cleaning his miniature tractor

it still felt defiled by its passage through Martha.
She gagged on Stretch Armstrong for over an hour

like pushing a latex lamb-shank through a shredder
but when, for his birthday, Jack got a Transformer,

an LED ball and a Night Sky Projector,
her belly lit up like a small Blackpool Tower;

she bleeped as she bled, on the toilet, in labour
with only a dead plastic *clunk* to deliver

and no one sends cards and a John Lewis hamper
when you shit out a Barbie then cry a bit after

or snip off the longest umbilical ever
to welcome a yo-yo baptised in excreta.

Why was the pogo stick gifted by Santa?
As snow fell outside, she was found by her partner,

a pool of blood darkly dilating beneath her,
muttering, 'baby, I don't know how it got there.'

The children were up way past their bedtime and had eaten more sweets than they could handle but it was a wedding so we figured it wouldn't kill them until my three-year-old tugged at my sleeve and said, 'The CIA are tracking me.' His eyes were bloodshot and it looked like he'd been drinking. 'They think I stole the codes,' he said. 'What codes?' I said. His voice clenched to a whisper. 'They've been sending me messages via the cake crumbs. I know it sounds crazy but toddlers disappear every goddamn day.' I couldn't help but be impressed by the sudden improvement in his vocabulary. Via? That was new. 'You're just tired, sweetheart,' I said. His whole body went limp. 'You're working for *them*.' 'I love you,' I said. 'Sure,' he said, wobbling back to the disco like a tiny heartbroken drunk, 'You're not even my real mum.'

every morning I am kicked out

of dream bed

and wake up in real bed

with your back to me

then blunder through the day in my rush

to get back into real bed

fall asleep and return to the dream

where you are waiting for me, naked, in bed

we don't have long

if the sheets start melting, that's our two-minute-warning

if your face blurs like cream, that's the end

I must turn my head slowly so as not to rouse

'am I asleep?' you say, referring

to your snoring self

'yes,' I say

'with your back to me'

you kiss your teeth

'I don't know what I'm missing'

the sheets start melting

hurry

your hand tracks down in the dark

like you're feeling for a rip

a little tear in the space-time fabric

just big enough to reach through

and touch your own body

asleep beside me

in the parallel world

which is kind of your kink – the hope

one night, you'll get so deep

your dream fist comes out my real cunt

which isn't possible

you know it's impossible yet

each night, you try

reaching

reaching

as your face blurs like cream and oh

god I'm going I'm going

## THE MURDER HOUSE

Even the estate agent tried to dissuade you.
The soundproof vault, the staircases leading
to nowhere, the firebrick kiln in the basement
with the scent of a surgeon's suite

not to mention your raccoon-eyed landlord
jangling all night around the strip-lit corridors
with an ogre's fist of keys hanging from his belt,
whistling whilst stacking Sellotaped towers

of meaty Tupperware into multiple chest freezers
but you said the rent was reasonable and moved
straight in. When I visited, your hair already
smelt of formaldehyde and something else

unplaceable but you said you 'quite liked it'
plus, the police had 'found nothing.' And when I
asked why a house needed twenty-seven chimneys,
you just blinked and accused me of 'being dramatic.'

After a while you stopped entertaining guests.
When I knocked, you slid the chain, claiming
to be towel-wrapped and fresh from the shower
although twice I saw your shoe in the door

and when I'd shout through the letterbox
'Sweetheart. Please. You're living in a murder house!'
you'd simply reply, 'Then why aren't I dead?'
and pad softly away on your transparent legs.

1) Don't want
2) Stop wanting
3) Hydrate
4) If your brain says, 'I want that,' disagree
5) Want cabbage
6) Breathe
7) Hold breath for one minute
8) Breathe again
9) Hold breath for four minutes
10) Want breath
11) Really want breath
12) Ask yourself, what *is* want?
13) Want is what?
14) Think of wontons
15) Keep holding your breath
16) Watch your watch
17) Wait
18) Pass out
19) Breathe
20) Come to
21) Withdraw life savings
22) Spend it all on one thing you hate
23) Love it
24) Love the thing
25) If your brain says, 'I'm skint now,' rejoice
26) Want nothing
27) Look at a tree
28) Be grateful
29) Look at a bee
30) Look at your knee
31) Look at the sea

32) Take pleasure in rhyme
33) Find a flea and look at it
34) Use a magnifying glass
35) Stroll around the city peering closely at small things
36) Pretend you're three
37) Think, 'Hey, three rhymes with tree, bee, knee and flea'
38) Guffaw
39) Get strange looks
40) Go home
41) Eat an unpeeled grapefruit, as an elf might eat an apple
42) Be, in a chair
43) Daydream of doing what you presently are
44) Do a mental body scan
45) Do it backwards
46) How are you?
47) Still wanting?
48) SQUATS
49) Make a delicious birthday cake for no one
50) Bin it, uneaten
51) Sleep on the floor for nineteen days
52) Want bed
53) Write a story about a pig who wears a chicken disguise
54) Write a story about an ostrich (or emu) stuck inside a church bell
55) Illustrate both lovingly, take months
56) Read them to a wall
57) Did the wall enjoy your stories?
58) No, your stories are meaningless
59) Sit with that
60) Eat a marrow
61) Catch a minnow
62) Remember bark rubbings?
63) Try these conversation starters on a beautiful stranger:
64) 'Isn't the word weird weird?' 'Hello, am I dead?'

65) Punch a pillow
66) Have full sexual intercourse with the same pillow
67) Think, 'Desire is the essence of identity'
68) Desire no identity
69) Hit yourself in the face
70) Harder
71) Harder
72) Want pain to stop
73) Stop hitting yourself
74) Relish the absence of pain
75) Willpower achieved
76) I said stop
77) I said stop hitting
78) Madam
79) It's just 75 steps, you're done
80) You can stop hitting yourself now
81) You're bleeding
82) Fucking stop it, will you?
83) Why aren't you stopping?
84) Please stop
85) Please
86) You're scaring me

I fantasize about writing you a suicide note.
Not the dying part, just the note. Imagine
a hand-addressed pearlescent envelope
placed on a mantel mere seconds before
the chair was kicked. No one's going to
skim-read that, are they? You'd memorise it.
Mentally underline. My family would ask,
'What did it say?' and perhaps you'd write
a poignant suicide poem in my style and
they'd print it on a commemorative postcard
whilst, secretly, you'd know the real note
wasn't fit for publication, wasn't trying to be
a poem, the note just wanted you to live
and be happy, an irony not lost on me.

Pete was in a bar called Ping
attempting to beat his girlfriend
at table-tennis
when our dad rang
to deliver his historic announcement.
His voice was strange
like he had a cigar in his mouth.
'I'm abdicating.'
'Advocating for what?'
Pete said, fitting his Bluetooth earpiece
before twirling his paddle
to smash a tiny ball.
'I, Terry the First, do hereby
declare my irrevocable determination
to renounce the throne.' It went on.
Something about 'a dying era'
and 'public opinion' but
his burger had arrived so Pete said
'Sure, whatever' and the line
went dead. The next day
he received three boxes via UPS
full of family albums
and school trophies
then Dad sold his house
and moved into a campervan
in the Hebrides with a retired
mathematician called Ralph
to live off-grid
which was fine by me
but awful for Peter
who hadn't read the small-print

disallowing descendants
all rights of succession
so now he'll never be King
or wield the sceptre
like Dad did
in his fearsome puffer jacket.

I ask my toddler
'What does a fireman do?'
        'Puts the water out.'
'You mean the fire?'
        He means what he means.
'You go around... with a firehouse,
        putting... the water out,'
he says, as if teaching
        etymology to a monkey.
'Sounds like a difficult job.'
        'It is,' he says
like he's got twenty years
        of service under his belt,
out there every night fighting
        water in his hard hat
with the fireman's logo
        (a giant droplet
with a cross through it) breaking
        doors, striding stairs
'Everybody out!' Aiming his hose
        of flames at a recently
poured bubble bath. Steam.
        Smoke. The disappointment
after minutes of fervent
        flaming when the water
still stands, just hotter.
        'I'm sorry,' he says
to the baffled homeowners,
        'This might take some...'
A crackle from his walkie-talkie:
        it's the Ocean Brigade,

the big guns, calling for
      additional units. 'Prepare
yourself,' says the boss,
      'It's fucking everywhere,'
and sure enough, when
      he gets home after another
long shift of exploding fish
      and slippery ladders,
his daughter's already up
      and dressed. 'Daddy,
why do you do what you do?'
      'Ask not why the plumber
picks plums, darling, or why
      the dentist builds dens.'
'Will you ever be *finished*
      though Daddy?
Will you *ever* put all the water out?'
      He looks down
at his scorched wet uniform,
      her clever little face;
plugs in his portable hairdryer
      and turns it on himself.

## STRIP LIGHT

No more loving in the dark,
that inky aquarium
where we could be anything.
Though we unplug the lamps.
Though we blindfold each other
with scented masks.
Still, our eyelids glow like neon lips.
Still, our breath particles
fall up around us like digital rain;
sighs become strobes,
fog lights then searchlights
scanning for cons
on the lam from themselves
as we squint hard against the back walls
of our brains, star-fished and wanting
to stay lost but dirty
socks flame on the floor now
like night vision snakes and each liver spot
tea stain on bedside mugs
makes itself visible, re-dressing the room
in separate details
like a nightclub at closing
or a glass booth in which
a new school receptionist
calls me 'the mother'
then turns to you, asking
brightly
'And you are?'

'I'm in the mood,' she says,
slotting in a pound
to free the trolley.
'What, here? In the Co-op?
Is there a toilet? Every aisle has CCTV?'
'No!' she says, activating
the sliding doors,
'In bed. Like normal humans.'
'That sounds incredible,
let's grab essentials and run home.'
'Onions,' she says.
I fling a net of three in the cart.
Maybe this could be a game?
Supermarket Sweep foreplay?
'Lovely plums, eight for paaand!'
'What?'
'I'm a cockney market trader.'
'We don't need plums.'
She stares intensely
at a probiotic low-fat yogurt
with '100% Grass-Fed Cows'
written in gigantic font across the pot.
'Glass-fed,' she says.
'What?'
'*Glass*-fed cows.
Wouldn't that be horrible?
Dripping blood from their big, trusting tongues?'
She holds up a litre of semi-skimmed
with both hands like a bottle of wine.
'This reminds me of my childhood.'
'It's milk.'

A crate of hot cross buns wheels past
and she bursts into tears.
I try to hug her.
'Hang on a minute there, you little perv.'
She ditches the trolley and strides
down the central aisle,
hissing over her shoulder,
'And what was all that weird kinky dogging stuff
about Co-op toilets and CCTV?
This is all about urges for you, isn't it? Grubby urges?'
'No, it isn't.'
'And now the desperation, running after me
like a stalker, holding a fucking stick
of garlic bread. I'm not aroused by garlic bread.'
'Neither am I.'
'So, I guess we're at an impasse.'
'A what?'
'An impasse.'
'We're not in a Greek tragedy.'
'Aren't we?'
She shoves her phone in my face.
'6.9 Million Dead. Does that turn you on?'
'No, of course not.'
My hands are shaking.
'We need space,' she says, marching off,
clasping a jar of light mayonnaise
to her chest like an urn,
'...and we also need vegetable crisps.'
*Vegetable crisps.*
The words yawn like a black hole,
sucking my eyes backwards
into my head until I see
my own brain glowing
like a radioactive cauliflower.

'Don't rise to it,'
I whisper, but it's hopeless,
I've risen like a body
from a tomb on Judgement Day,
shaking off the soil, queuing
with the other corpses in the aisles
between our stones. 'What's going on?'
says one corpse.  'I dunno,' says another.
'Must be *time*,' says another.
'Oh good,' says another. 'Oh shit,'
says another. 'Don't worry,' says another,
'anything's better than being down there.'
'Yeah,' I say, crunching the leaves
like vegetable crisps beneath the remains
of my feet. Then
the queue halts.
'False alarm. Back in the ground.'
So, we all get back in our graves
and close our eyes
but we can't sleep now
we're too awake.

is held in Spectorlake, Arkansas. Every year, the motel signs rearrange their letter-tiles, 'Welcome Druggettes!' and our minibuses arrive to tourniquet bunting and 'Nodding-Out Gnomes' whimsically placed on each lawn: drinking from dog bowls or face down in dirt. The diners advertise 'Overdose Buffets' and there's even an icing sugar snorting competition for the kids who call it 'Summer Halloween' and greet us, stage-coughing, their little nostrils crusted in ketchup.

We always have a big reunion the night before, embracing old friends and registering our addict names with the committee. Meth Mouth Molly. Wet Brain Bill. Junkie Jeremy. Or something more subtle and arty like Detox Shampoo Dave or DJ Drunkorexia. The judges are looking for three things: Visual Appearance, Physical Motion and Inner Darkness, or I.D. 'Can I see your ID, babe?' is an industry joke yet the sad fact is few can sustain it on stage; sobriety reclaims their face for one second, a tell-tale flicker of dignity round the eyes next they're sobbing in the wings, healthy pink stripes down their jaundice paint.

Newbies soon learn there's more to addict impersonation than tattoo track marks and Pot Noodle fasts. True self-hate takes years to master like the Handstand Scorpion Pose in yoga, or jazz drumming, and any Druggette worth their salt (or 'worth their coke' as we say in the biz) knows you can't win without it. Abscess Alf lived on the streets outside his condo, begging for change. D.U.I Danielle deliberately lost custody of her children and wrote a blog about her experience which inspired me so much that, *this* year, I'd thrown my life's savings at a Brazilian heart doctor to teach me a show-stopper.

Silence in the theatre. Spotlight on me. I just had to not believe in myself. I focused my mind, replayed my mantra: you're shit you're shit. Yes. Yes, I am! *Perfectly-executed Pupil Constriction moving seamlessly into Blue Lips landing in Crumpled Position rounded off with an Actual Death.* Ten seconds. Twenty. I surpassed all rehearsals. Afterwards, the judges clocked it in at two minutes and called it the realest routine they'd ever seen. I don't remember much more of the night, just spidery sunspots, but the first thing I saw when I opened my eyes was the Golden Needle Trophy on my hospital table and Mum and Dad crying with pride.

## BLESSINGS HEAPED UPON BLESSINGS

At seventeen, I took a pill
with my face on it
and fell down the swollen hole
of my left pupil, emerging
at an altar dressed in white
beside a woman
the priest called 'First Wife'
but my mum seemed happy
so I drank champagne
in a hot-tub flecked
with petals like floating clots
and noticed I was wrist-deep
in a colleague, 'Where's my wife?'
I asked after she'd come
but she looked strangely hurt,
throwing my balled socks
into her drawer
like puppet fists
so, for years, I was imprisoned
in that flat, just loafing
to the freezer for ice cream
until her waters broke
and I slipped on the puddle
missing the birth
in A&E, the doctor said
I definitely had a substance
in my system but it could just be
someone else's blood,
'Your right arm is burgundy,'
she said, holding two syringes,
'While your left is hot pink'

like the fingernails of the valet
who tossed my Ferrari keys
'I can't drive,' I said, crashing
through factory doors
where workers were clapping
from the cages of forklift trucks
so, pension secured, I retired
to a vintage cottage
where Third wife wept
in bed all day, propped
on flowery pillows,
her brow mantled with veins
like a Victorian Strong Man
straining to lift a boulder
and when I finally said
'Is it something I've done?'
she stared with such
contemptuous bafflement
I never asked again
till I was old and bound
to a rotating chair bed,
swivelling and scribbling
exclamation marks
into a fat leather diary:
*Jan 1st: Change your life!*
*Jan 2nd: Watch out*
*for that falling chandelier!!*

## HOW WAS EVERYTHING

The
vulture
circles
like
a
waitress
on
rollerskates
asking
have
you
finished
with
that?

Stop screaming. That's not your job.
You are choosing to choke on my hand
until you're blue in the face.
Even if I'm hurting you – and it's a big if –

you are *choosing* to choke on my hand.
Control means letting go.
Even if I'm hurting you – and it's a big if –
'Argh' is a statement of intent.

Control means letting go.
You think lungs entitle you to breathe?
'Argh' is a statement of intent.
'Ouch, ouch, you're strangling me.'

You think lungs entitle you to breathe?
Dishonest people use phrases like
'Ouch, ouch, you're strangling me.'
You have the shoulders of a supplicant.

Dishonest people use phrases like
'Why are you doing this?'
You have the shoulders of a supplicant.
Choose a single suffix.

Why are you doing this?
*Because* you can't be 'ing' *and* 'ed,' can you?
Choose a single suffix
to usher you into the prostrate phase

because you can't be 'ing' *and* 'ed,' can you?
Let's call it 'final edits'
to usher you into the prostrate phase.
Are you willing to cease inner monologing?

Let's call it 'final edits.'
What I'm hearing is, you're wailing.
Are you willing to cease inner monologing?
When life offers you an out, take it.

What I'm hearing is, you're wailing.
Don't call it death, call it 'un-me time.'
When life offers you an out, take it.
I was in the grocery store the other day, yelling

'Don't call it death, call it 'un-me time!'
You don't look willing.
I was in the grocery store the other day, yelling
'Must I keep repeating myself?'

You don't *look* willing.
Stop screaming. That's not your job.
Must I keep repeating myself
until you're blue in the face?

The slogan on the iconic poster
is *Harvey Wallbanger is my name and I can be made*
which is funny because after drinking
ten Harvey Wallbangers, my parents had sex
against a wall and made me. I neglected to ask
if that meant twenty or five each. According
to folklore, a Californian surfer called Tom Harvey
took one sip of orange juice, vodka and Galliano
shook up in a highball glass then banged his head
against a wall. Or got so drunk he started running
into walls. Or finished his drink and, bereaved,
headbanged the nearest wall. Mixologists
call it *Something sweet and tangy that'll make you
crawl later*

I was loading the dishwasher when the clinic rang.
'I don't know how to say this,' she said,

which seemed a strange opening
sentence for a medical professional,
'...but did you use a sperm donor three years ago? Vial 2360?'

'Yes,' I said. I didn't particularly like thinking
about the donor. It wasn't something I thought about.

'Well – and we've had several meetings
about the protocol around this – it's unprecedented, you see...'
She sounded like she was vaping.

'Obviously we vet all our donors, there's a long form,
we meet them in person but, of course, we can't know
what they will go on to do... in the future.'

'What do you mean?' I said.

'He's... The Radiator Killer.'

I put the rinse-aid down.

'You know,' she went on, 'That man
who chained those girls to boiling hot radiators
then cut out their tongues and led them around on leashes
like dogs? The police called us, apparently, he donated sperm
to multiple clinics over a period of thirty years.'

I grabbed my laptop, searching 'sperm' in my emails.

'Did you say vial 2360?'

'It's a shock,' she said.

'We used 2361.'

Her voice was replaced by Vivaldi's Four Seasons.
I pressed start on the dishwasher.

'Okay, thanks for waiting.
2361 is a completely different donor,
please disregard everything I've told you, have a nice day.'

'Wait... did 2361 do anything bad?'

'I'm sorry but I'm not able to divulge private information.
I'm sure he's lovely. Excuse me,
I need to make another call.'

In Truth or Dare, if everyone picks truth
it's undaring to pick dare. Sam went first,

tucking his chin as if recoiling from
his own kiss. 'I stomp on snails in the park

because I love the crunch,' he said, going
big too soon. Silence. I couldn't bear it.

'Oh Sam,' I said, on everyone's behalf,
'*Everyone* massacres snails for pleasure.'

In truth, I'd never dream of such a thing
but I wanted to make him feel normal.

Jo next. She'd self-published a children's book
featuring a foul-mouthed vulva called Slash.

'Don't be embarrassed, Jo!' I said, 'We've all
penned a tale about swearing genitals

for the under-five market. I wrote one
about a singing severed penis called

Hop-a-long.' I hadn't obviously
but Jo looked at me with a kindred warmth.

Bob's turn. 'Relax, Bob!' I said, 'Everyone
showers with their sister as an adult.'

I felt I was playing two games at once:
Truth plus this sport of mindless empathy

I'd invented. 'Who among us has not
stolen a bottle of liquid morphine

from our cancer-stricken mother-in-law,
decanted it into a Fanta can

and sipped it during our niece's wedding,
Christina?' The room swelled with acceptance

like a sedated hippo giving birth
in her sleep. And just as I was starting

to lag, counting heads, thinking how many
sins were left to falsely claim as my own,

Sam jumped in. 'Oh Paul,' he cried, '*Everyone's*
filmed a homeless man drowning in Skyros.'

Have we? I thought. Bob and Jo both avowed
'We *all* let our toddlers play with unwashed

anal beads so chill out, Elizabeth.'
I couldn't tell if they were serious

but the mood had turned competitive, wild;
everyone striving to boldly confess

or personally relate to the worst things
possible. 'Anne, sweetie, who *hasn't*

shared a taxi with their best friend's rapist
after a book launch since she wasn't there

and splitting the fare was cheaper?' High-fives
occurred, people joined in: neighbours,

meter-readers, door-to-door canvassers:
'Everyone hates the poor' and 'everyone

chokes women.' Anne begged for a second go,
forgetting the time she'd 'king-punched' a deer.

Whatever the admission – hit and run,
elder abuse – someone in our cohort

would scream 'me too!' or 'snap!' I longed to draw
a circle around my feet with a stick

of chalk, to mark some kind of mystic wall
between me and this orgy of awful

confessors, cheeks greasy with laughter, eyes
black as melanite. Then it was my turn.

'Say anything,' they said, 'We've all been there.'
Had they? This group of colleagues and strangers?

I pictured them lounging in the background
of my gravest errors, mouthing 'go on'

like extras in a recurring dream,
my chorus line of negligent angels,

jaded from centuries of witnessing
firstborns slain on slabs, palpable darkness,

locust-swarms thick as bombproof doors, who now
mooch the earth, shrugging their wings, handing out

little business cards printed with halos
to humans bad enough to forgive them.

## CUCKOO

My doctor said to swim
when my meds wore off
so I rented a locker,
pulled a smooth suit
over my lumpy body
and accidentally tiptoed
smack-bang into Senior
Aqua Fit and before
I could escape saying
sorry my mistake, they
beckoned me in and
for an hour we failed
to keep time with the land-
locked instructor urging
us to move our legs
and arms in right-left ways
through treacly water but
my God were we trying
like wooden cuckoos inside
glued-shut cuckoo clocks,
thwacking our little heads
against little doors like I *will*
chirp my solo, I *will* strike
the hour, I *will* snatch
a second in the light.

## DOT AND MAUD

After three decades of bed death, it's a shock
to find our technique much improved
like we're graduates of a thirty-year night
school with modules on clenching and moaning.
What's got into us? Who are these hijackers,
wrestling the yoke from our dozing crew,
piloting us into the sun? Did you see that?
Our souls ejected from our bodies, now
entwining above us like tandem skydivers
or the enormous gloved hands of a Spanish
puppeteer, let's call her Dolores, who when
walking one day in despair for her life, spotted
two old puppets gazing blankly from a bin
and seized upon us, crying, 'They're perfect.'

## ACKNOWLEDGEMENTS

Thanks to the editors of the following journals and anthologies in which these poems first appeared, a few in slightly different versions: *Poetry Review, After Sylvia* (Nine Arches Press), *Iterant, Poetry London* and the *TLS*. Also, I borrowed the title 'Old Man Home Phone' from the podcast 'Knowledge Fight.'

To Michael Schmidt, whose ongoing belief in me is baffling and restorative.

To Andrew Latimer, Jazmine Linklater, John McAuliffe and the whole Carcanet team.

To David Godwin, Philippa Sitters and Rachel Taylor.

To Laurie Bolger, Andrew Cracknell, Seanna Fallon, Sarah Gillespie and Maya C. Popa for their friendship and support.

Inexpressible thanks to my son's brilliant other mother.

To my parents and my brother. I love you all, always.

To my beloved friend Rachel Long, the person to whom I can send new poems without dying of embarrassment. Our poetry chats (and everything-chats) make me glad to be alive.

For Reece, for lending me pieces of his brilliant imagination. I am so proud to be your mum.

And finally, to my beautiful wife Eliza – the most incredible step-mum – for understanding why these poems are so much darker than our daily lives, and that fears of loss are love poems too. Also, your feedback is always bang on. I love you, and Reece, utterly, ridiculously, endlessly.